Gilead's GoblinZ™

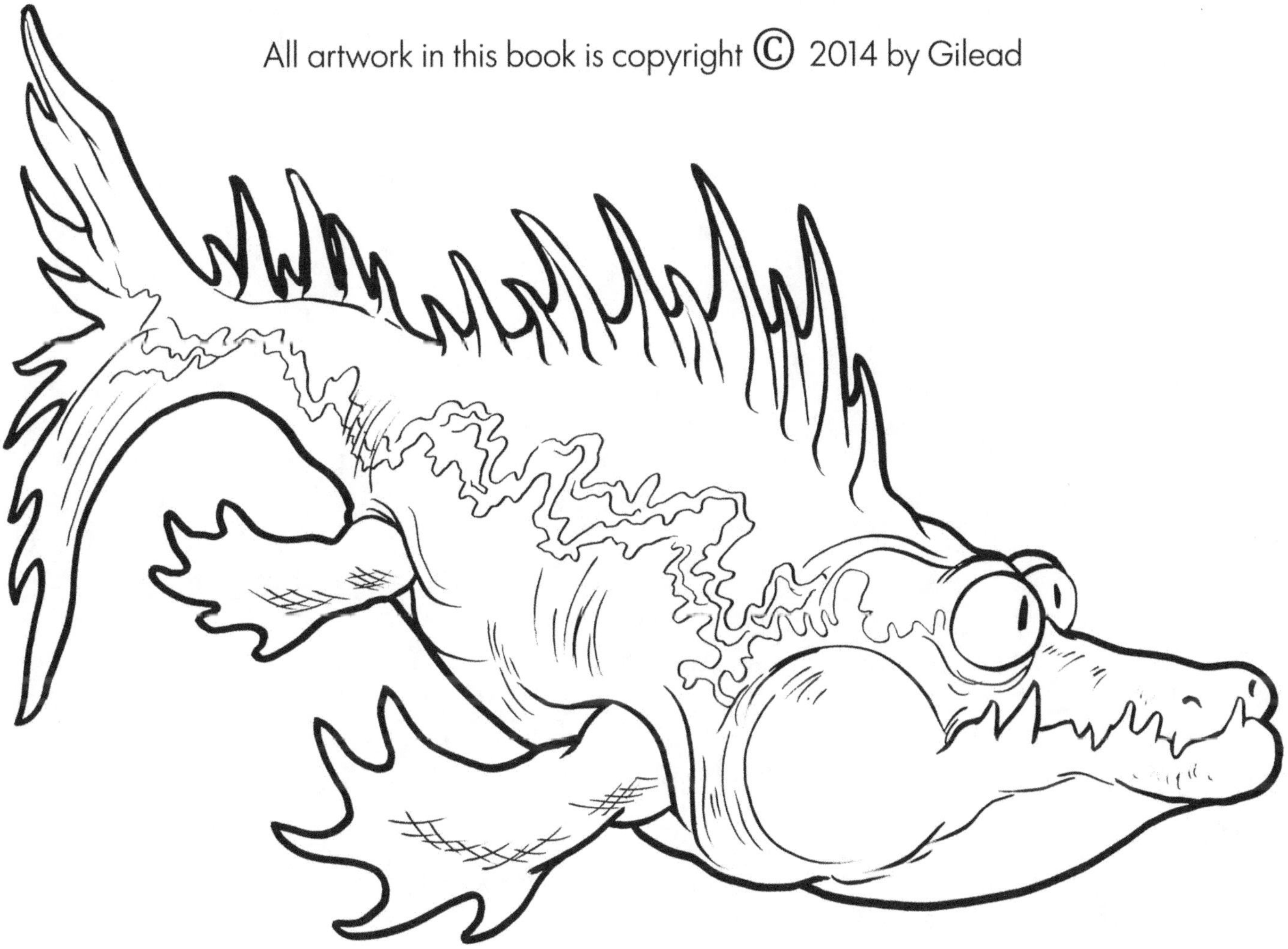

Made in U.S.A.

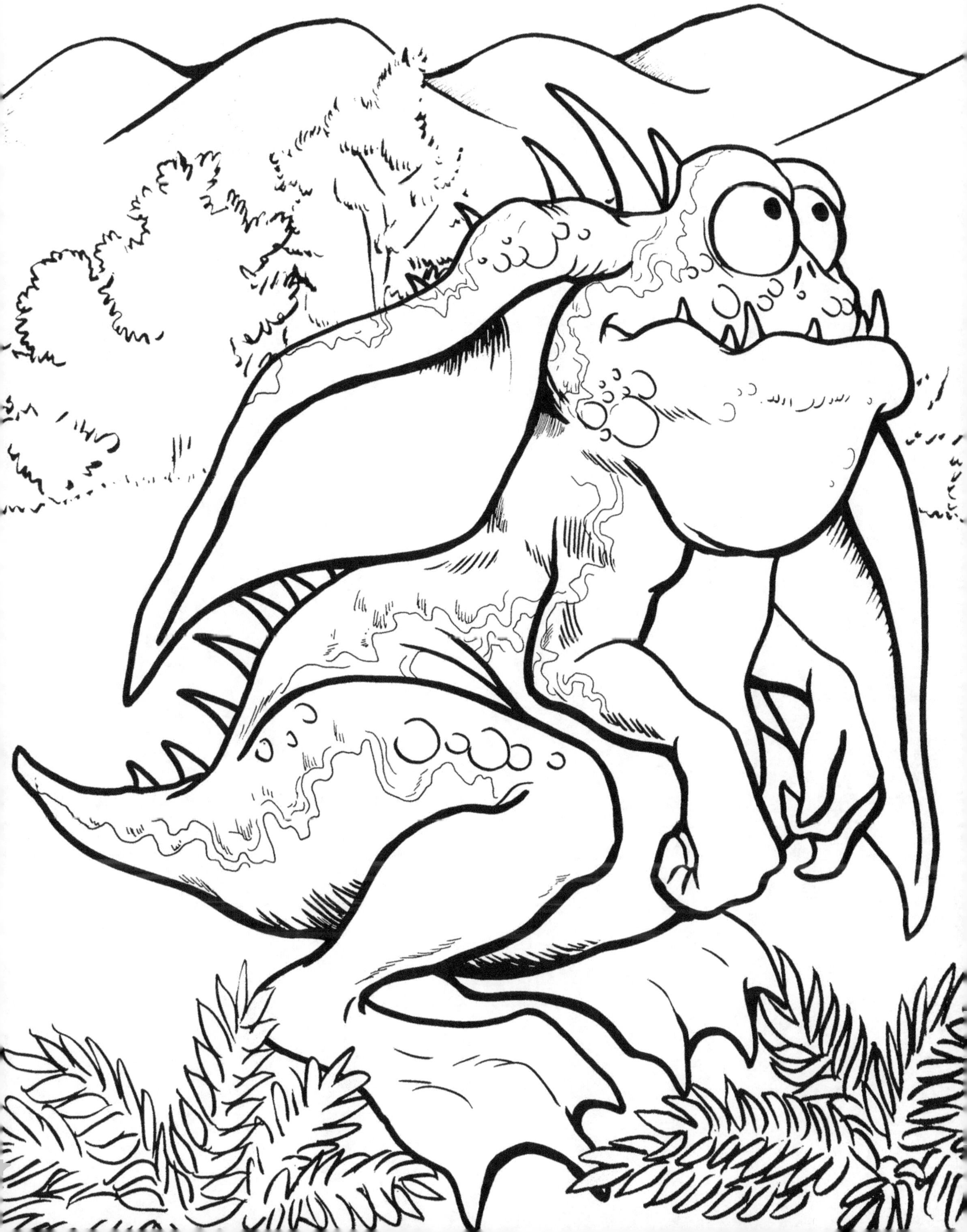

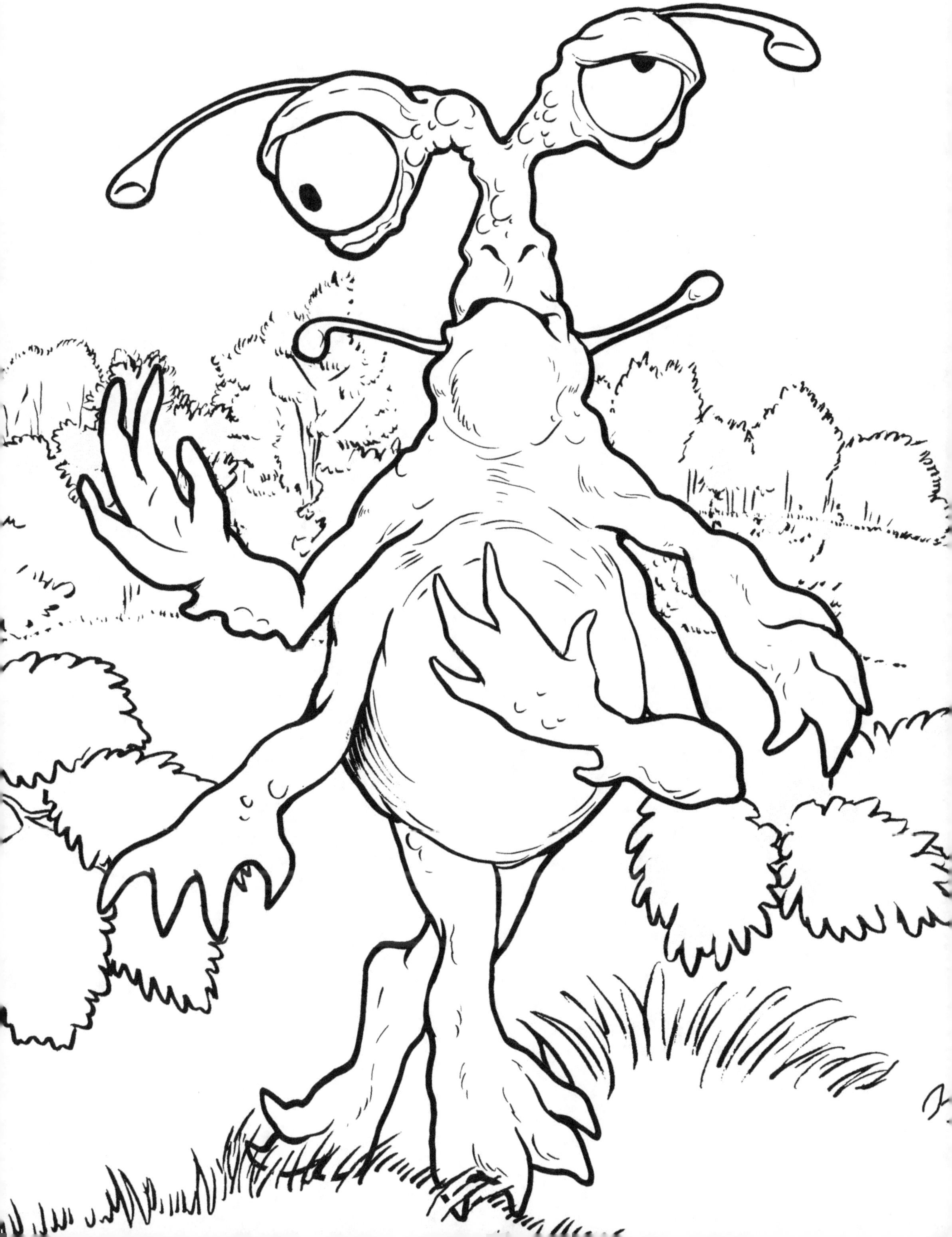

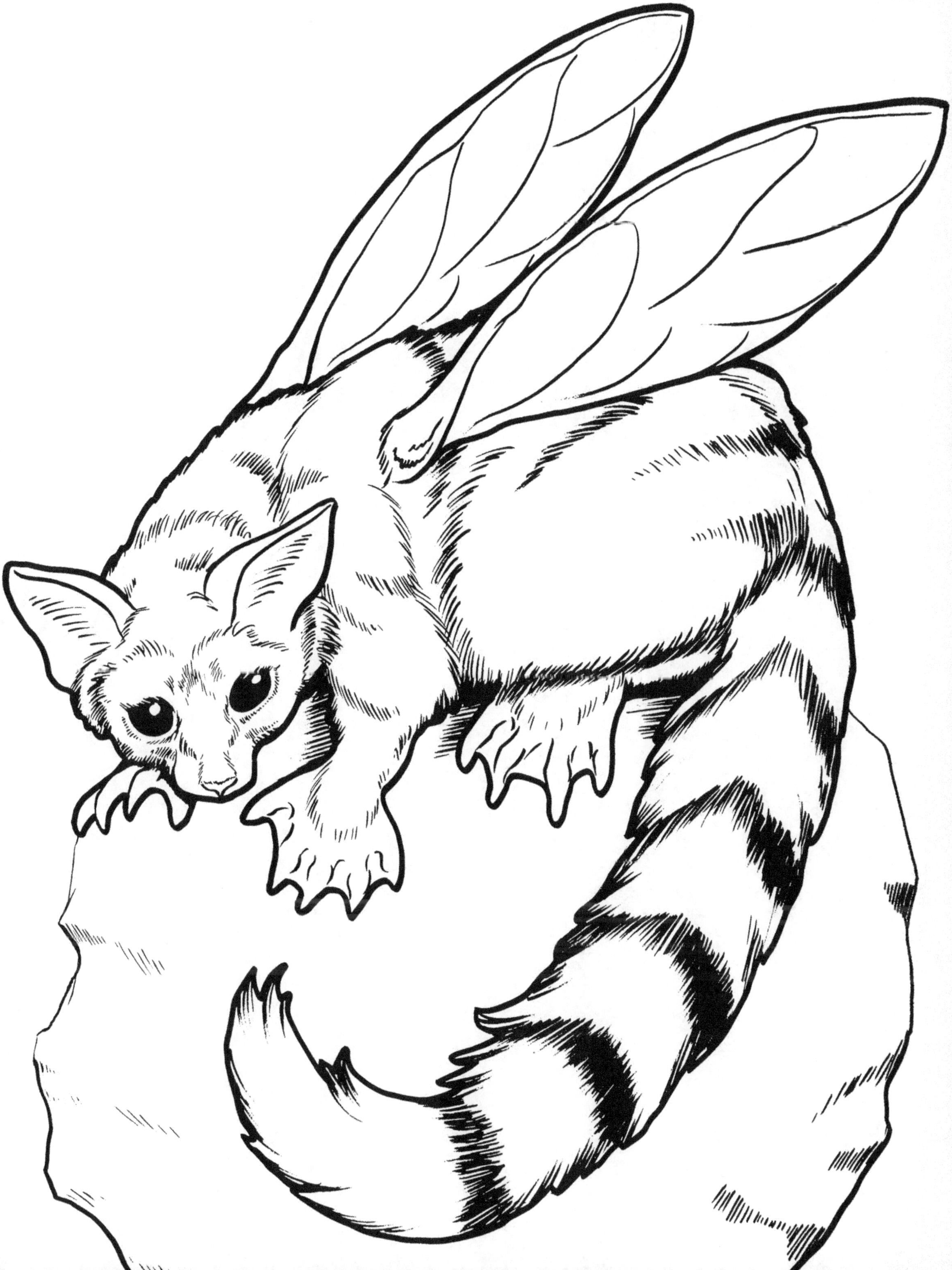

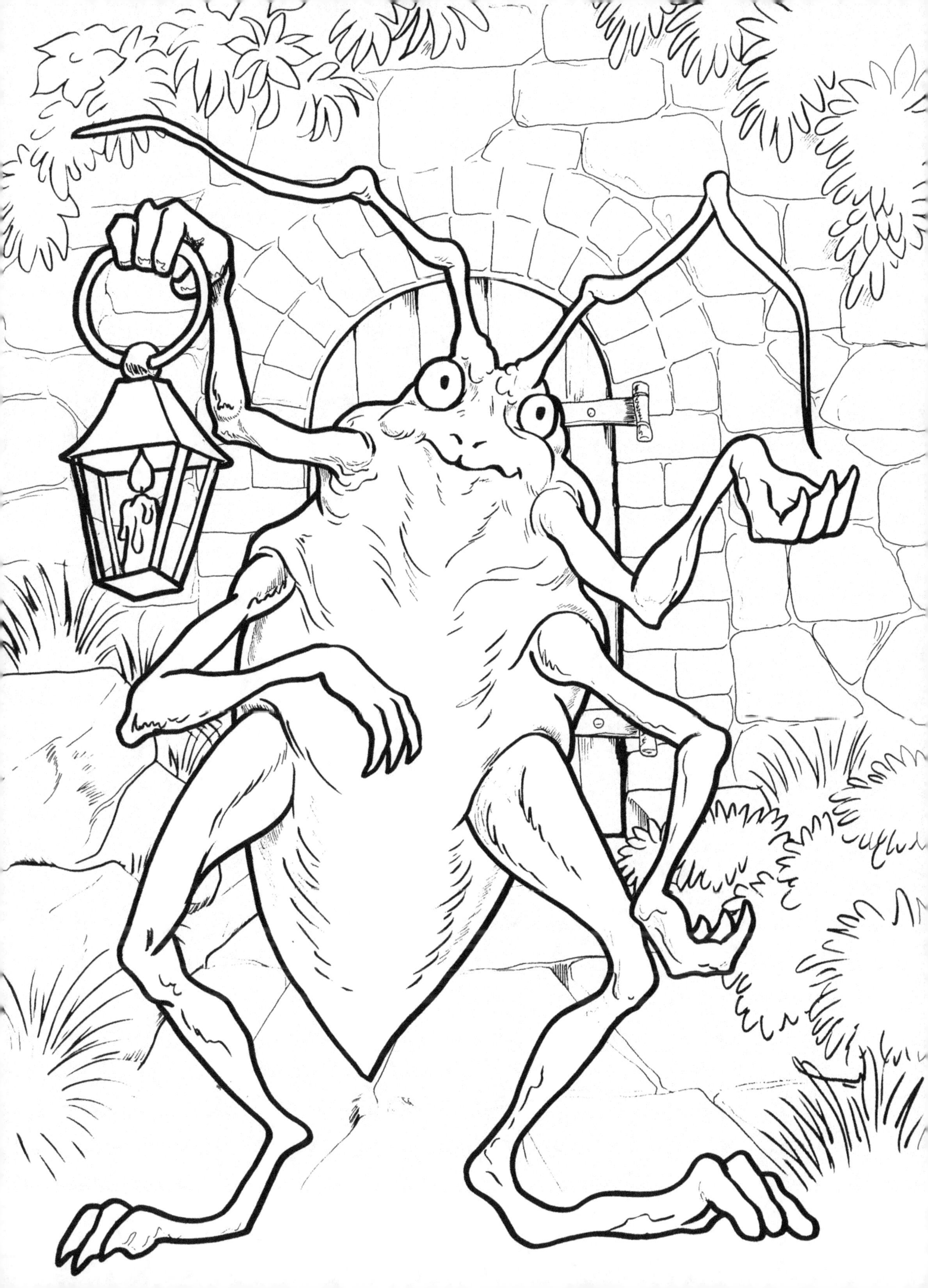

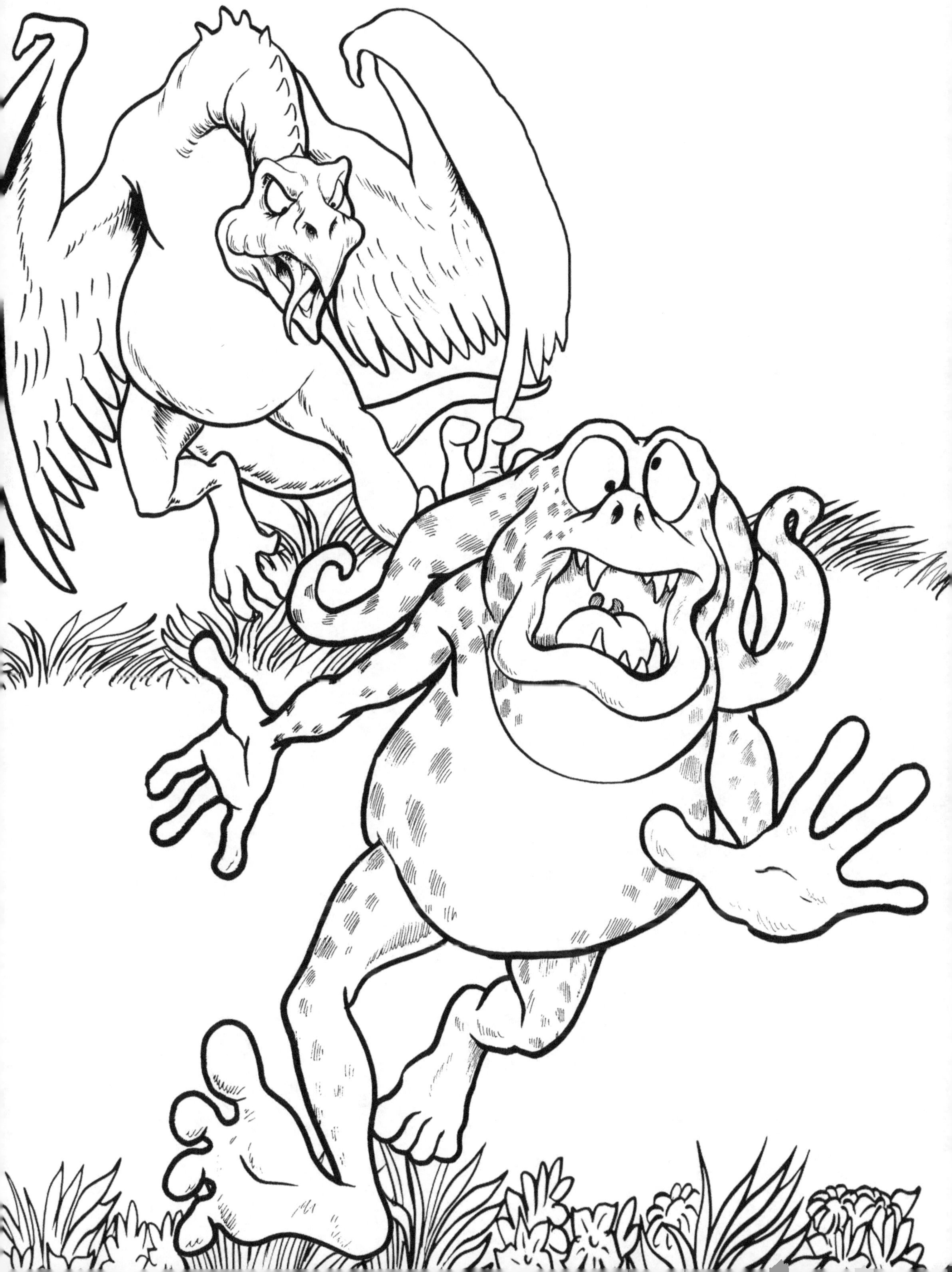

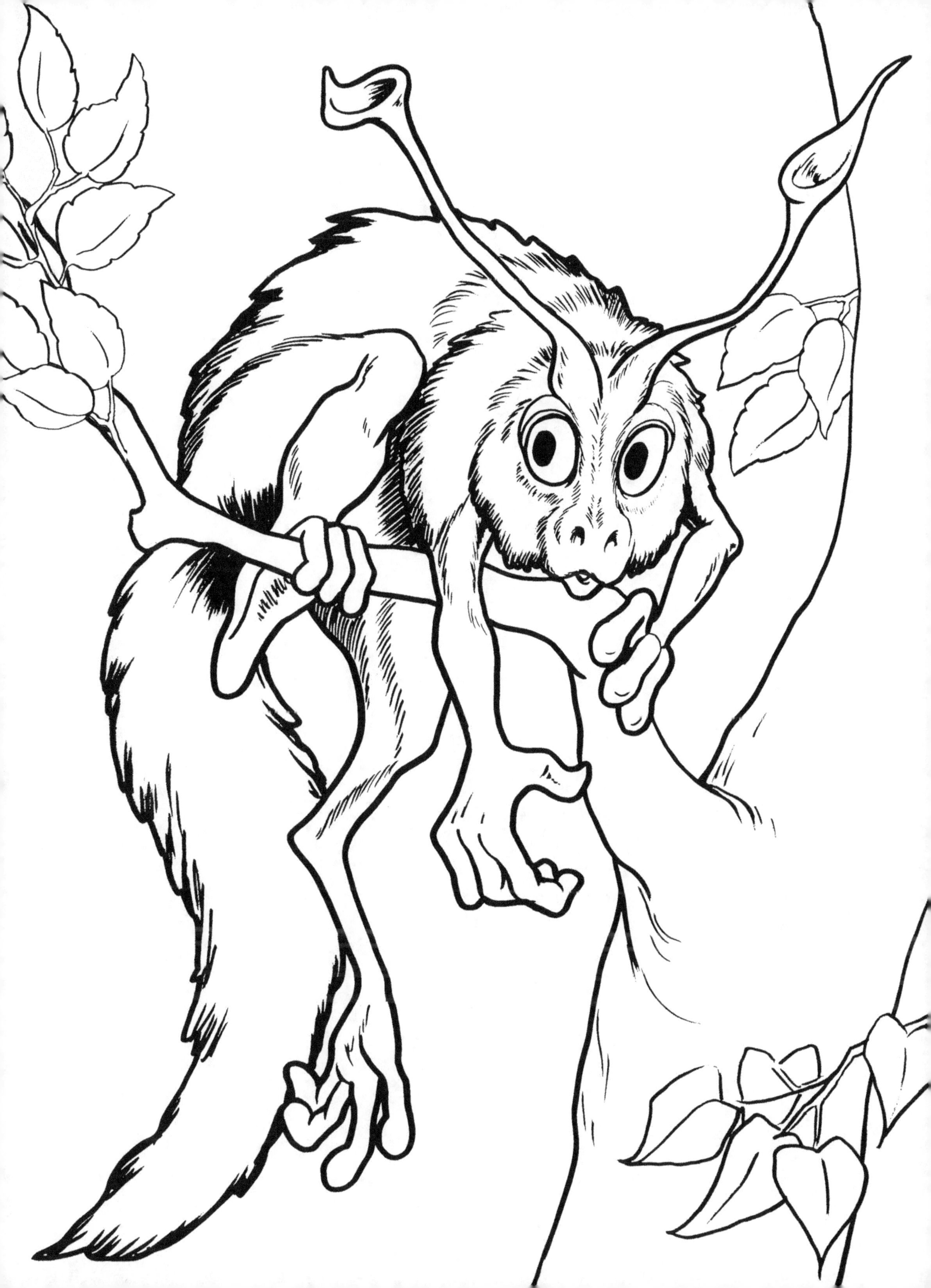

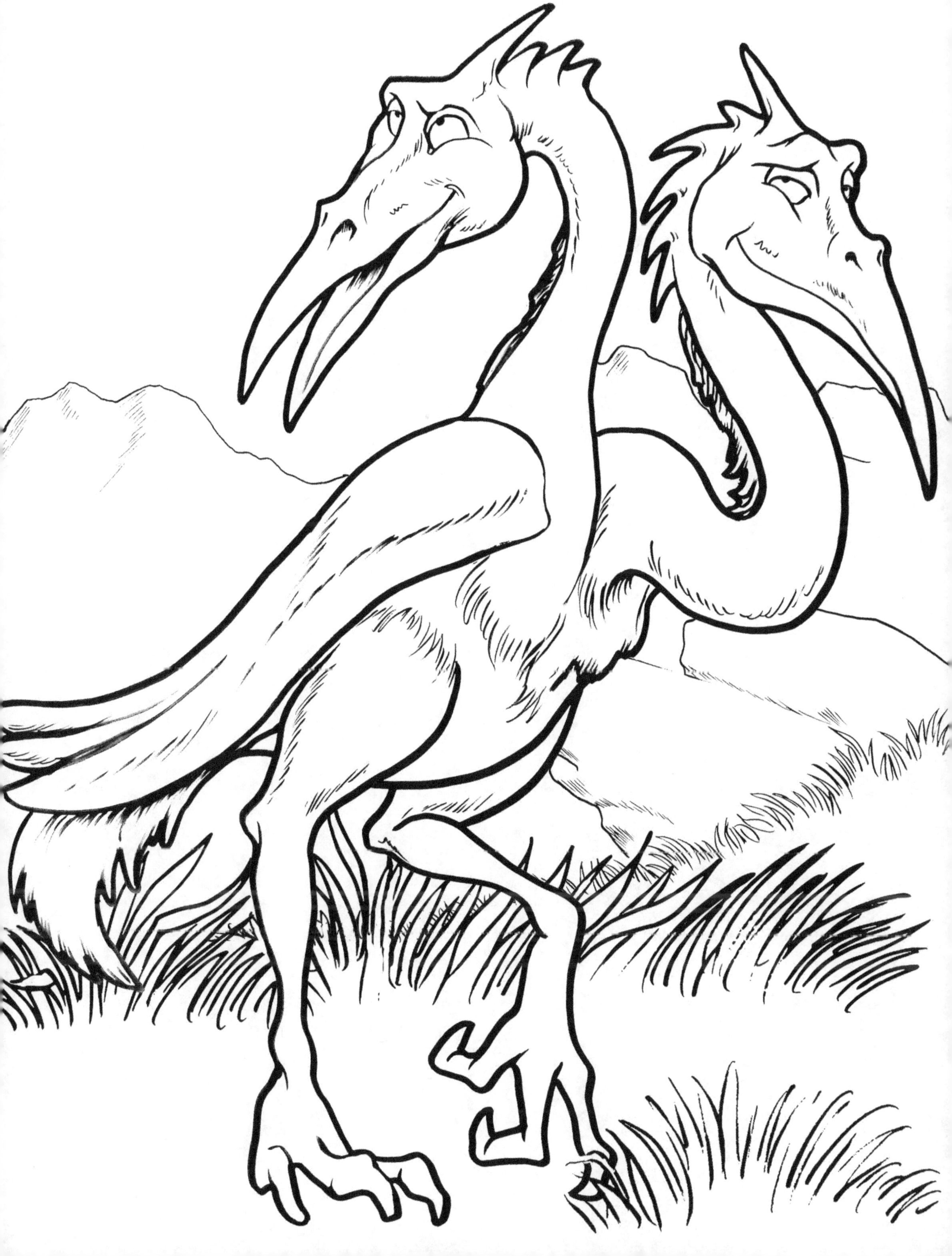

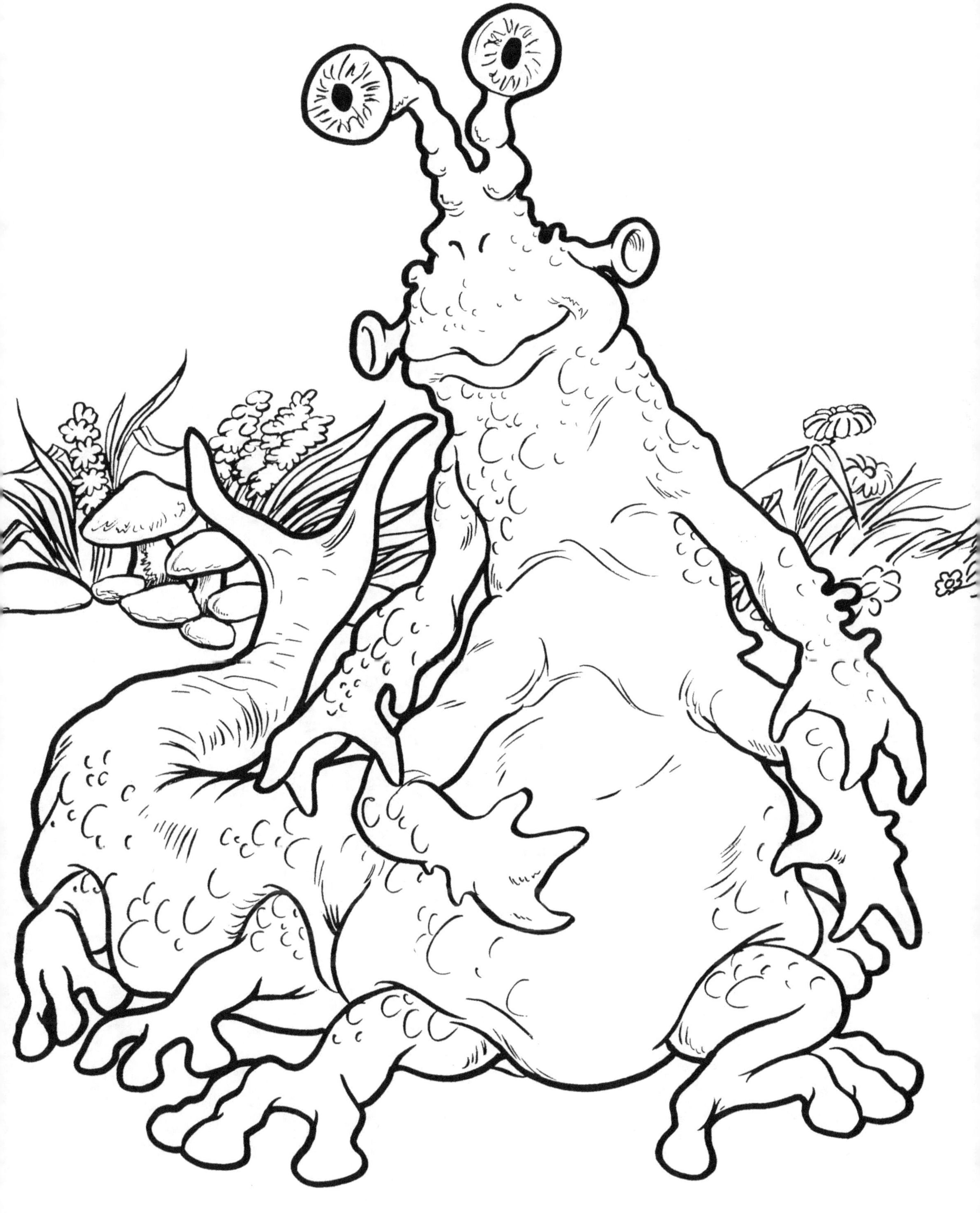

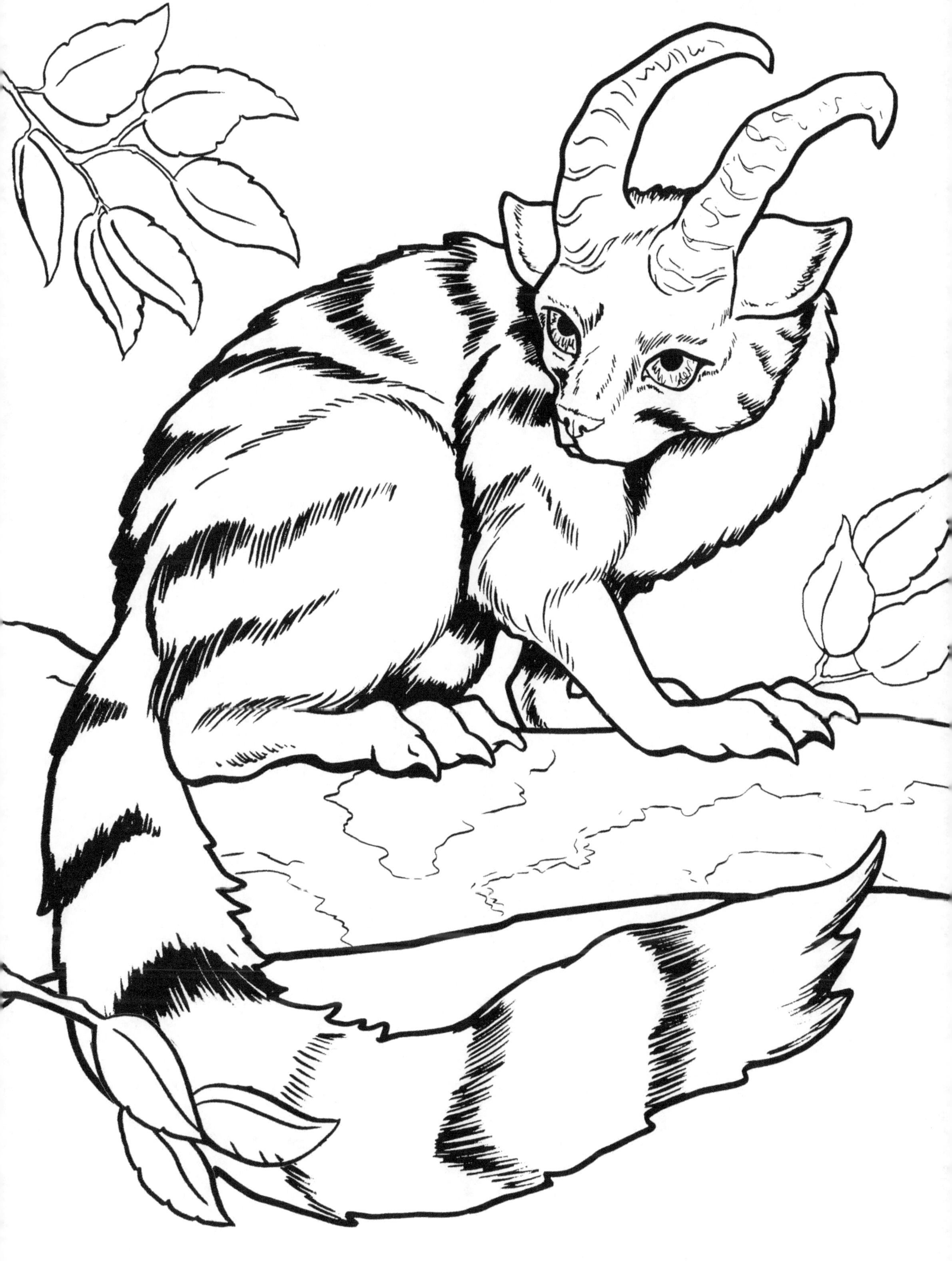

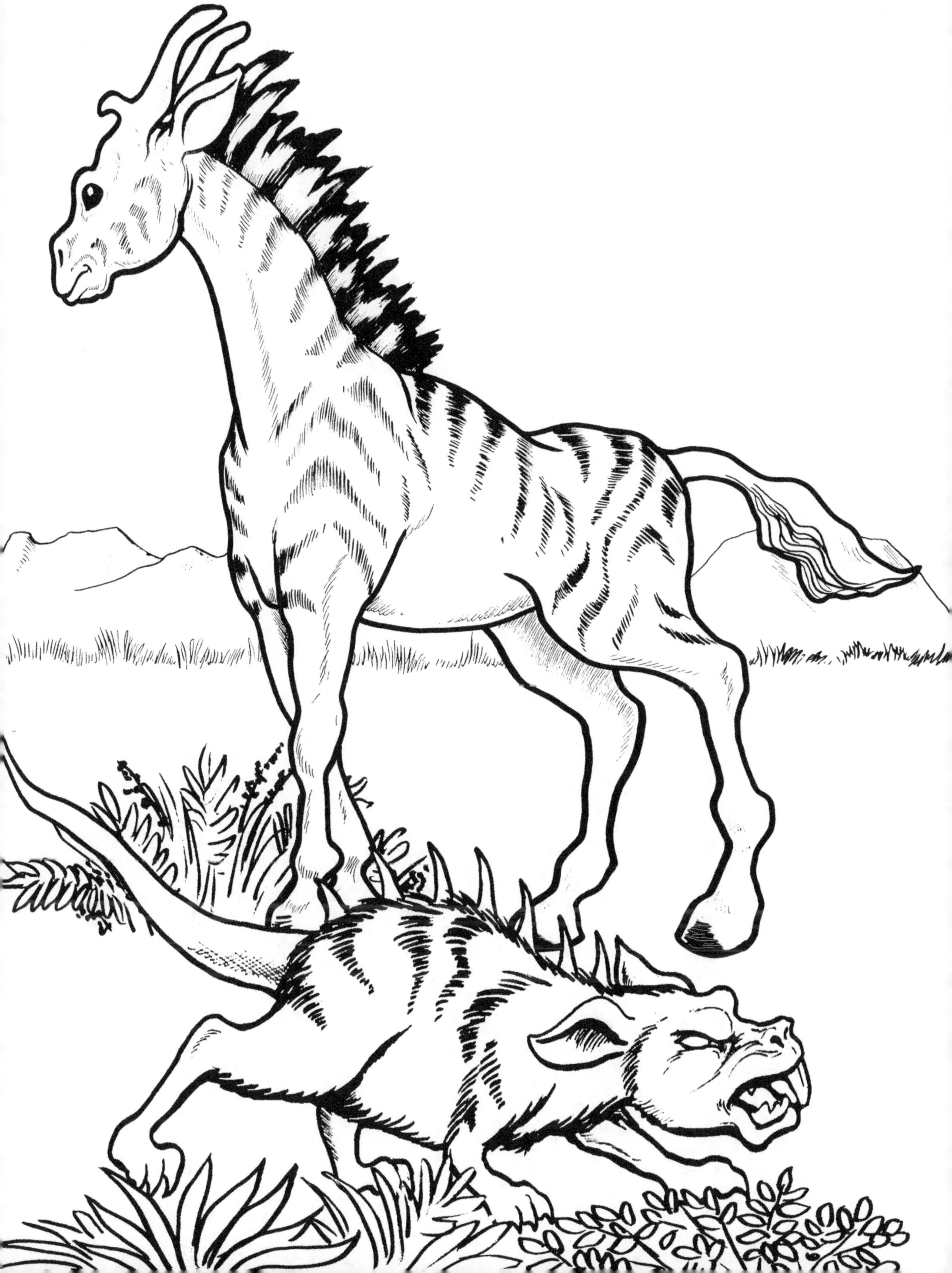

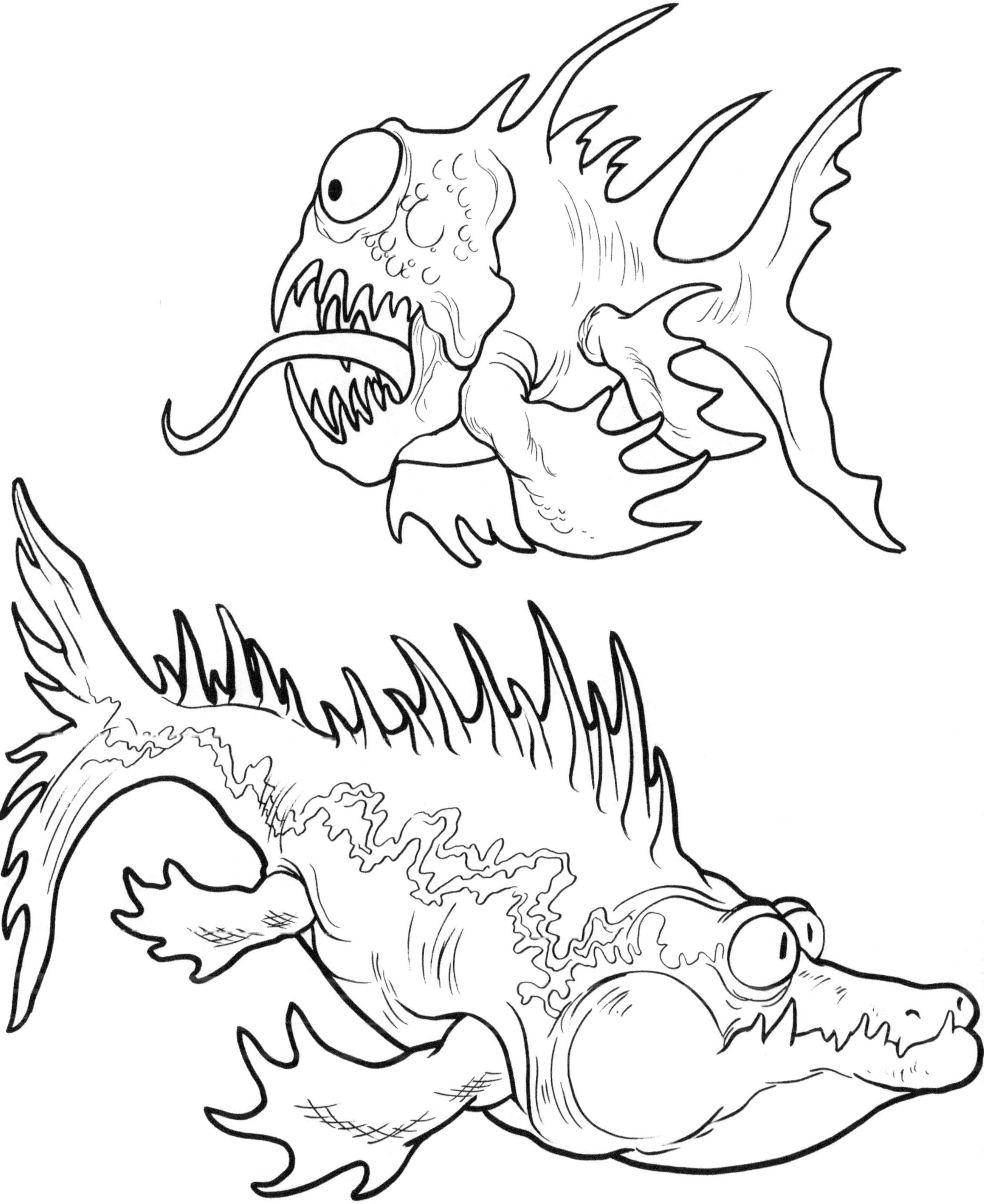

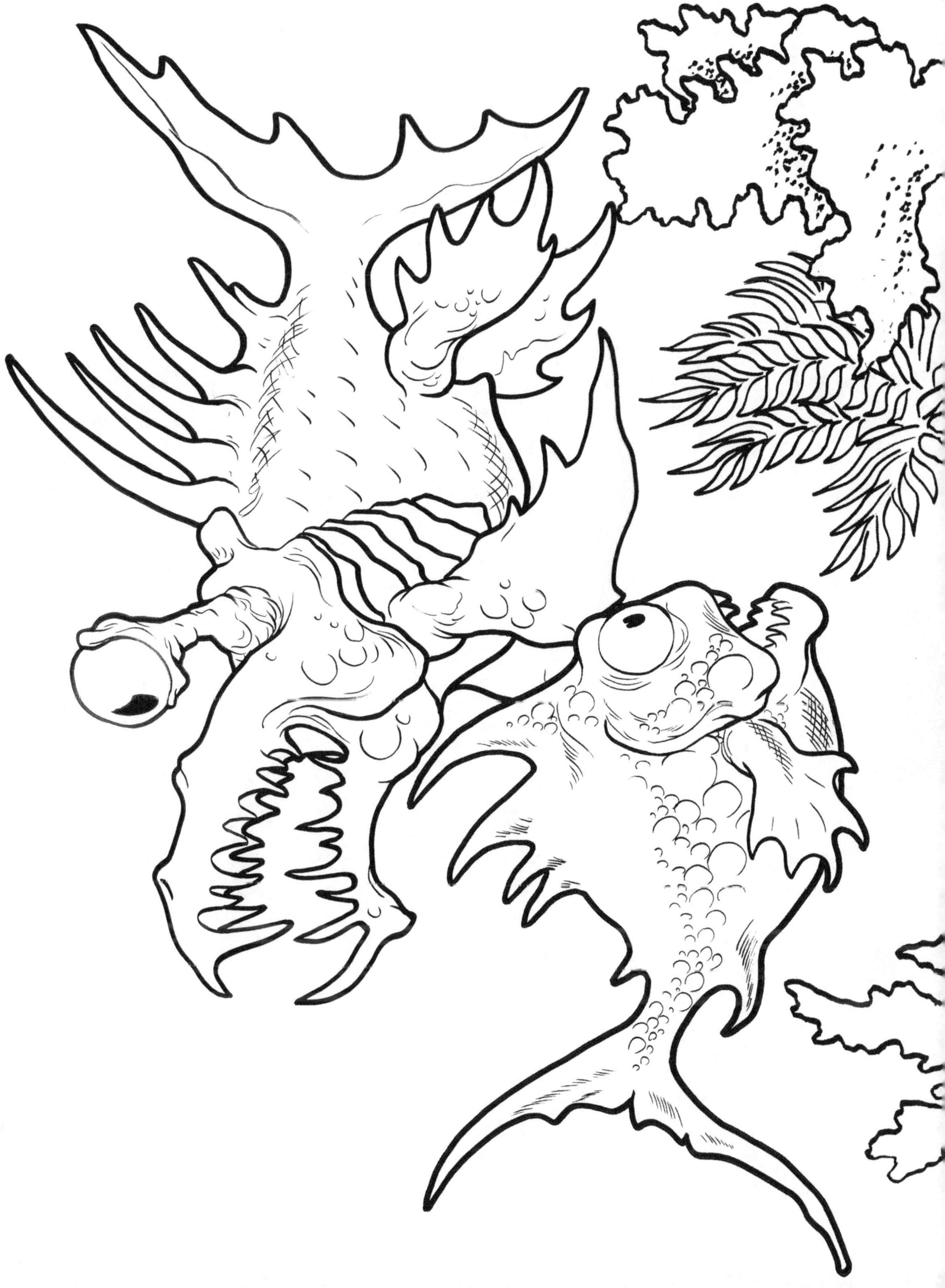

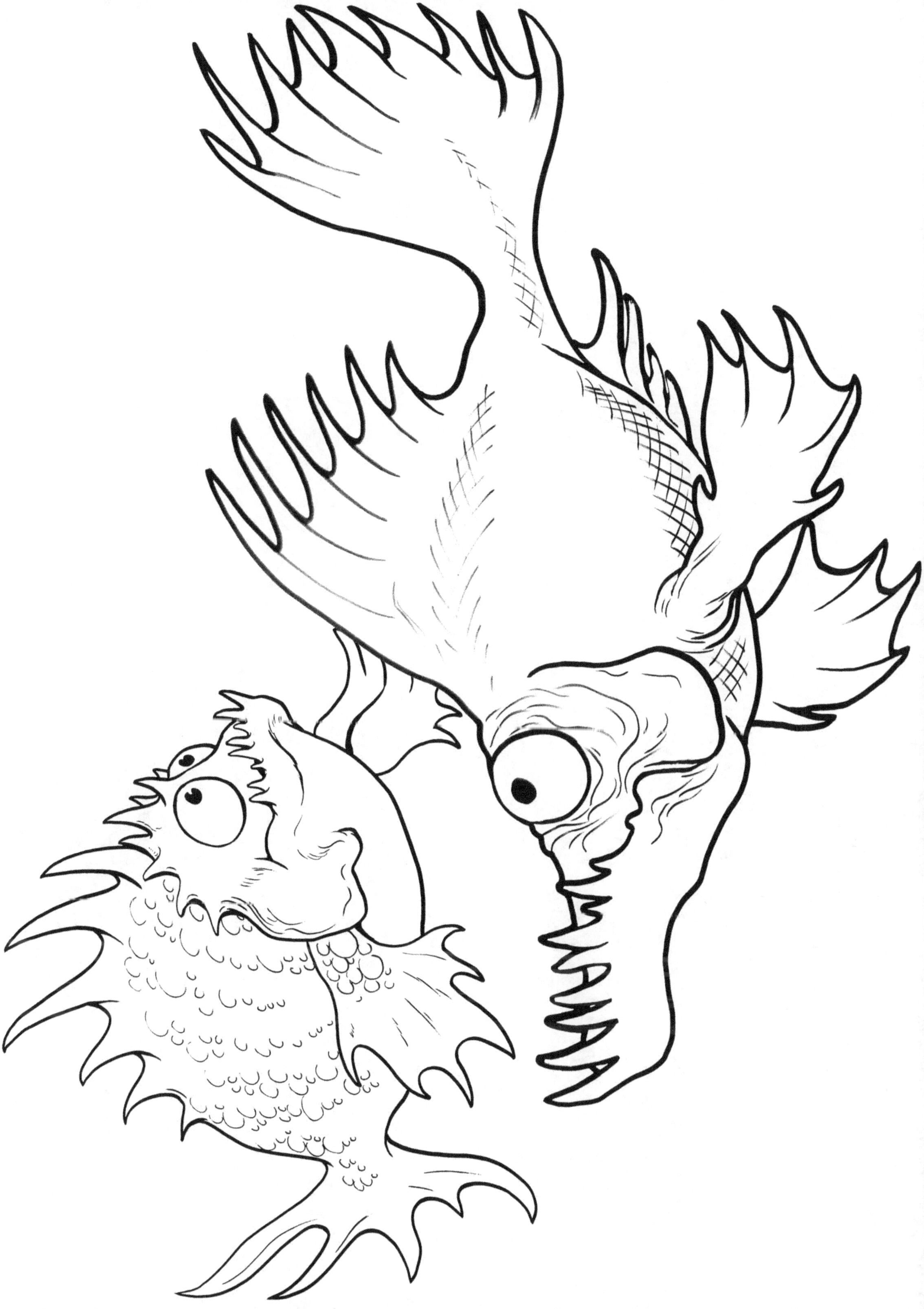

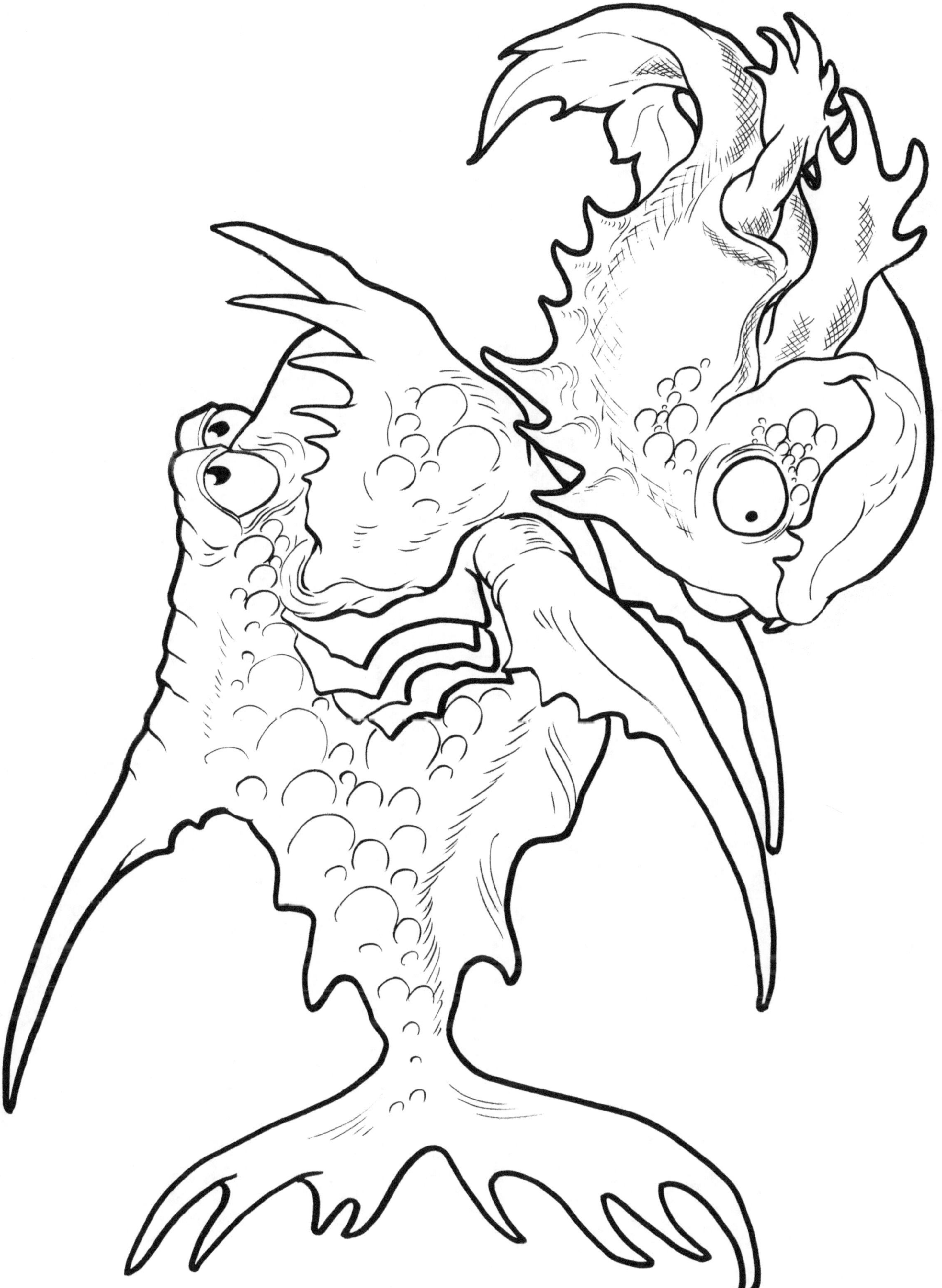

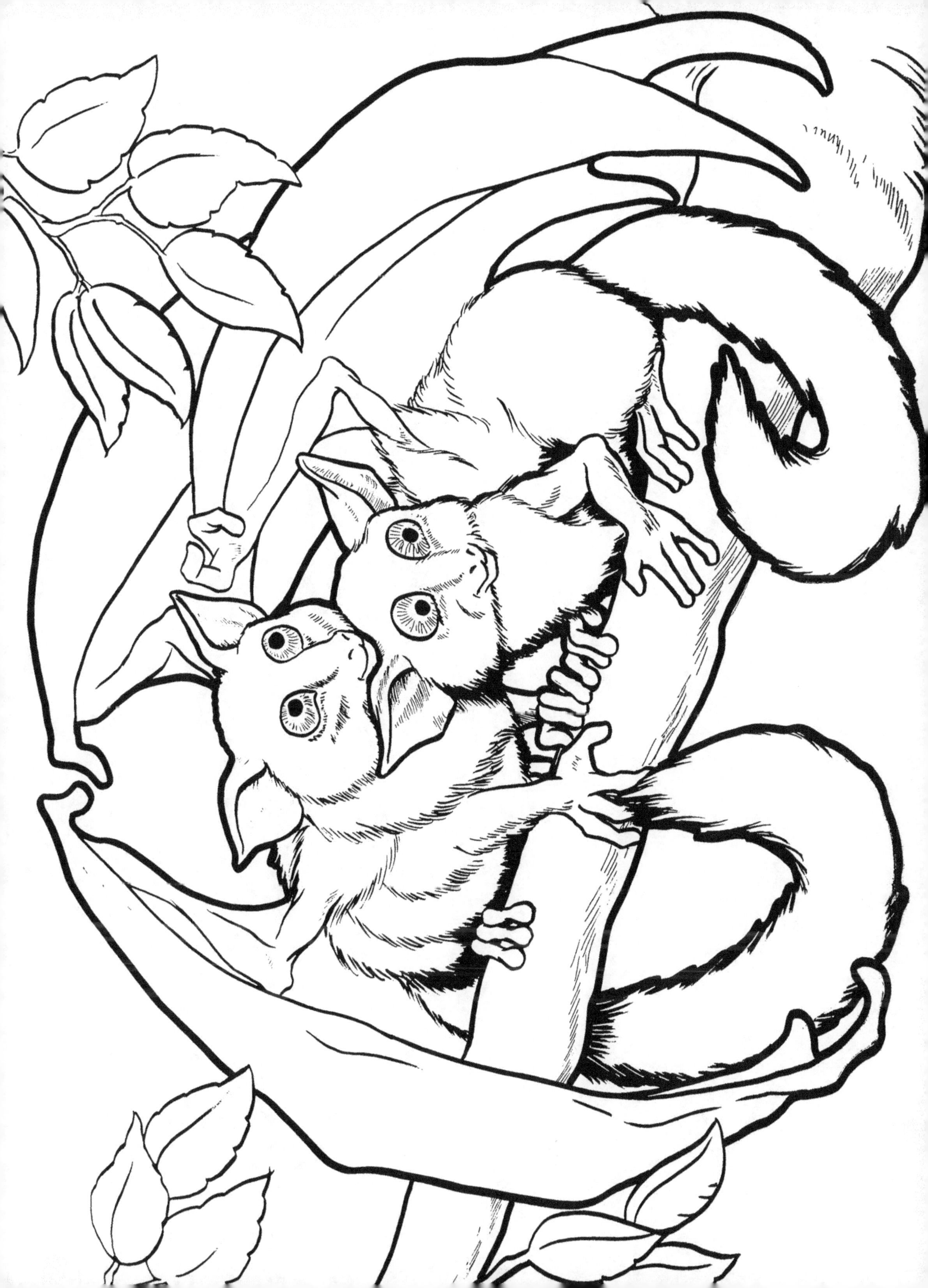

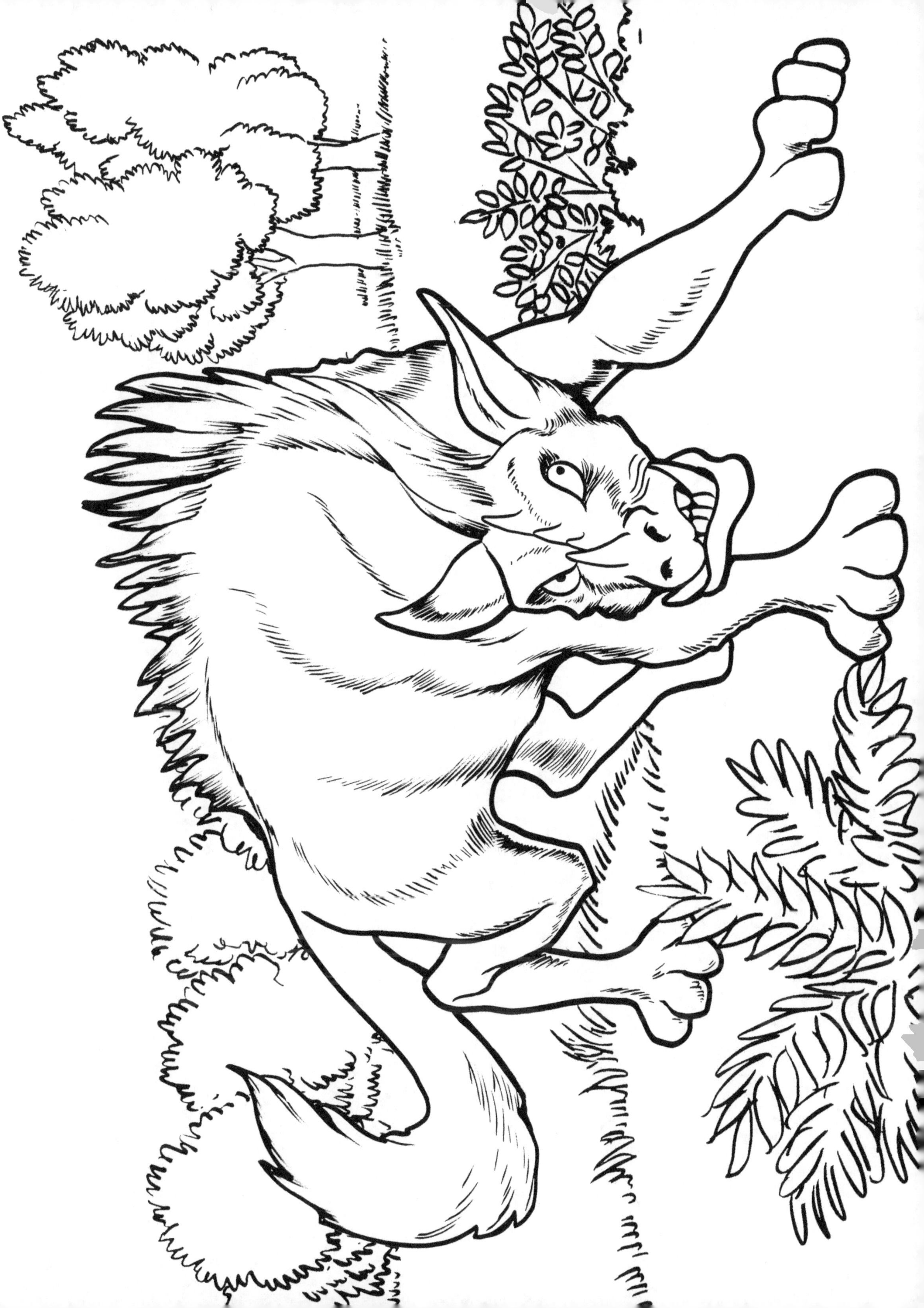

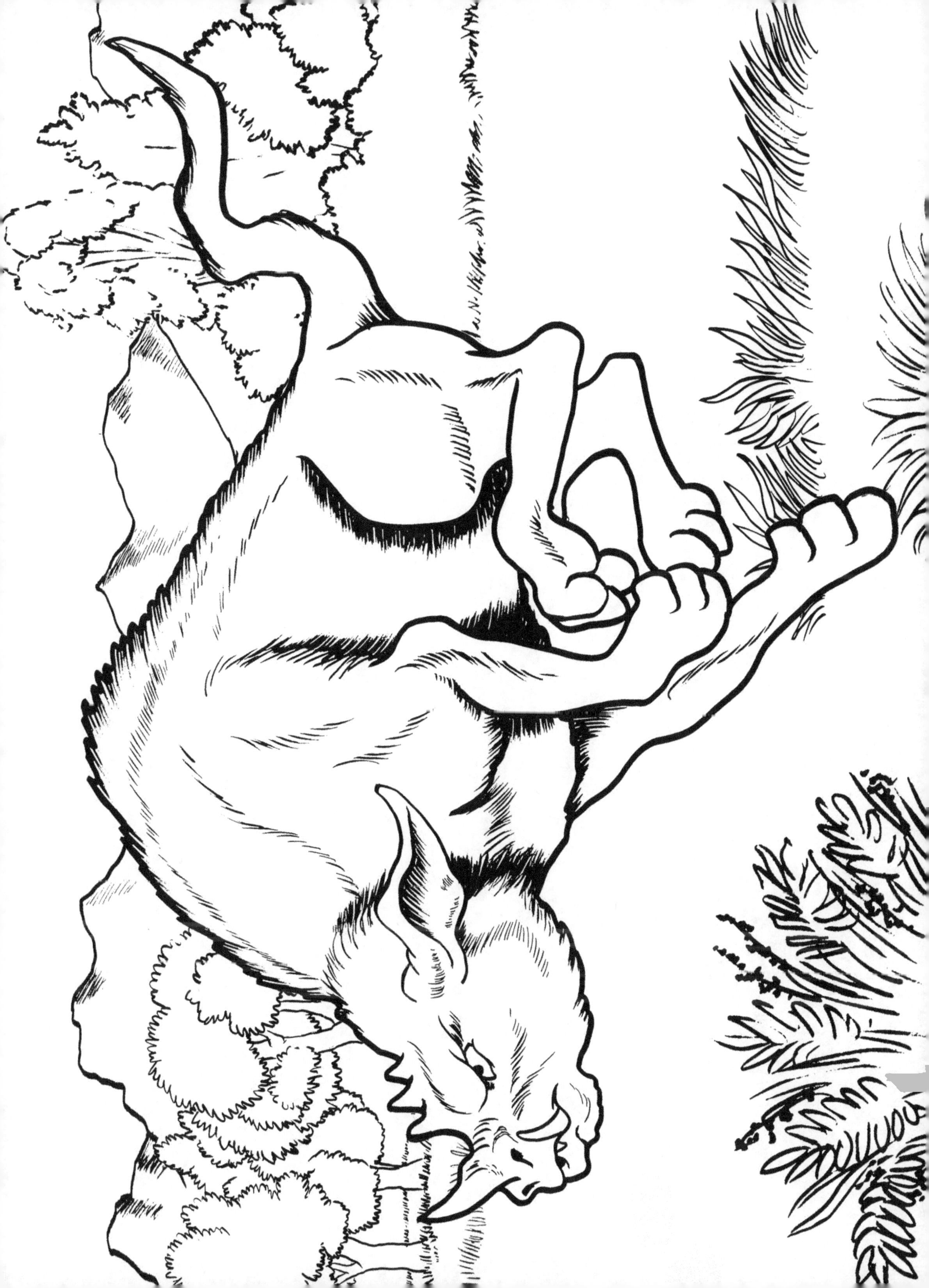

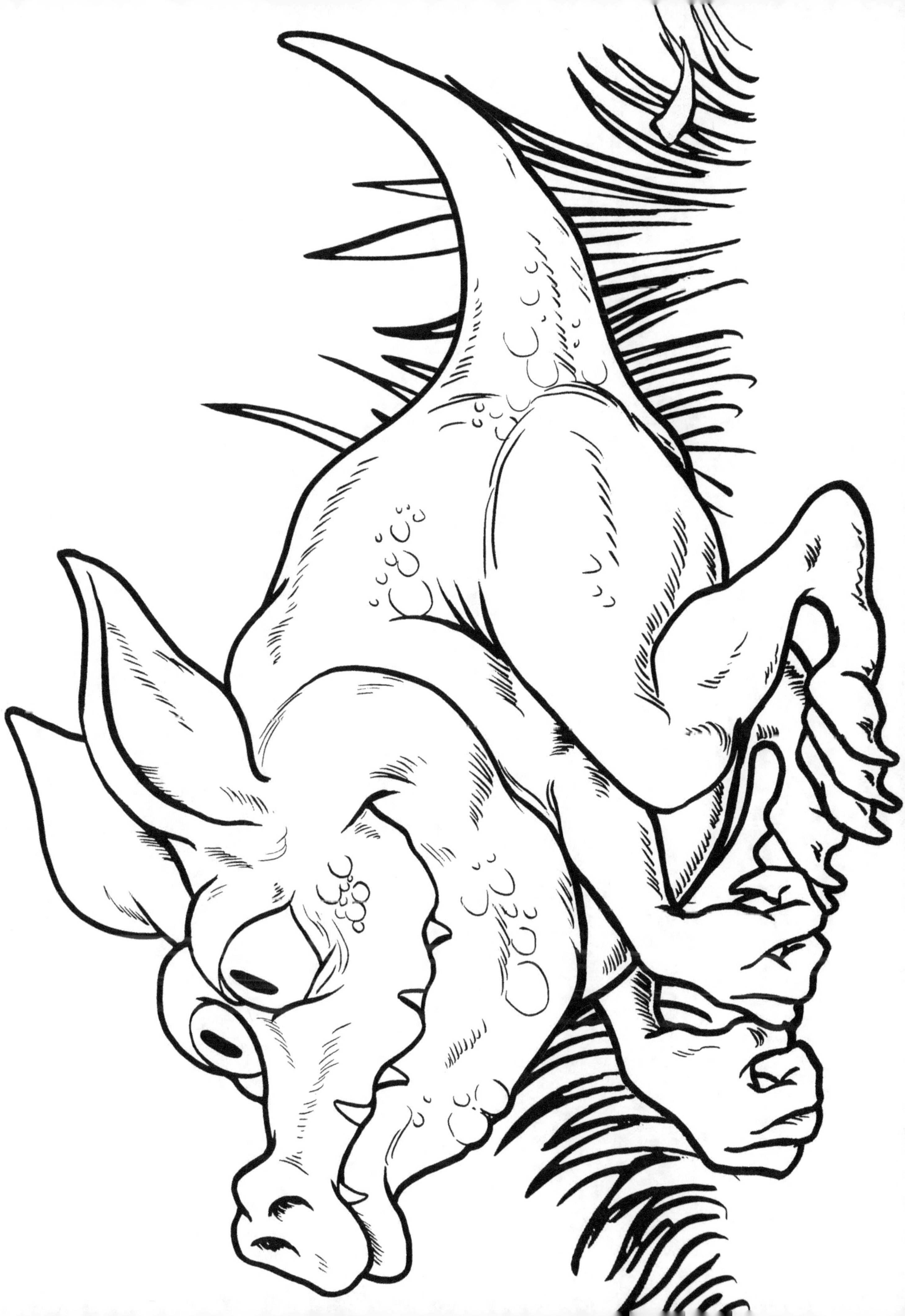

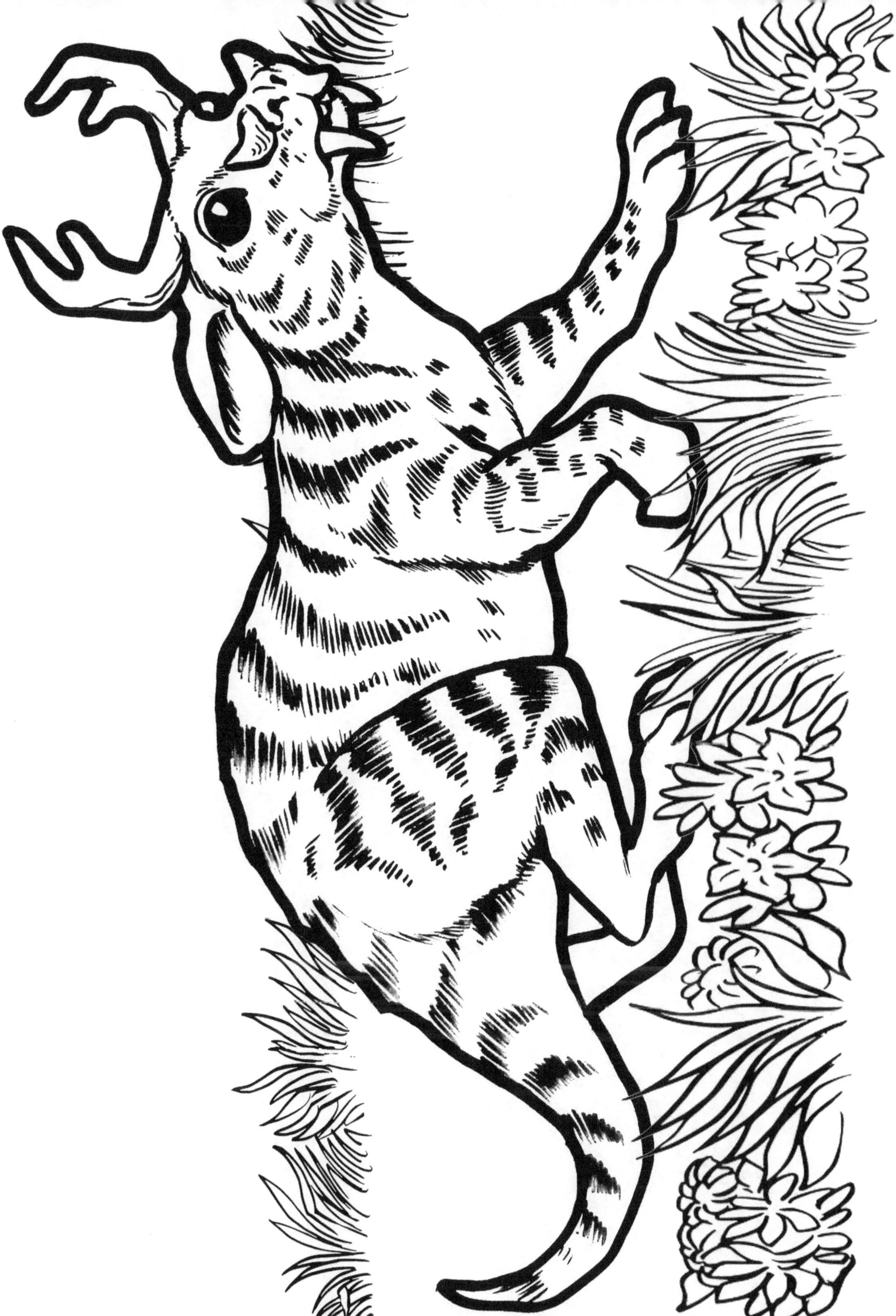

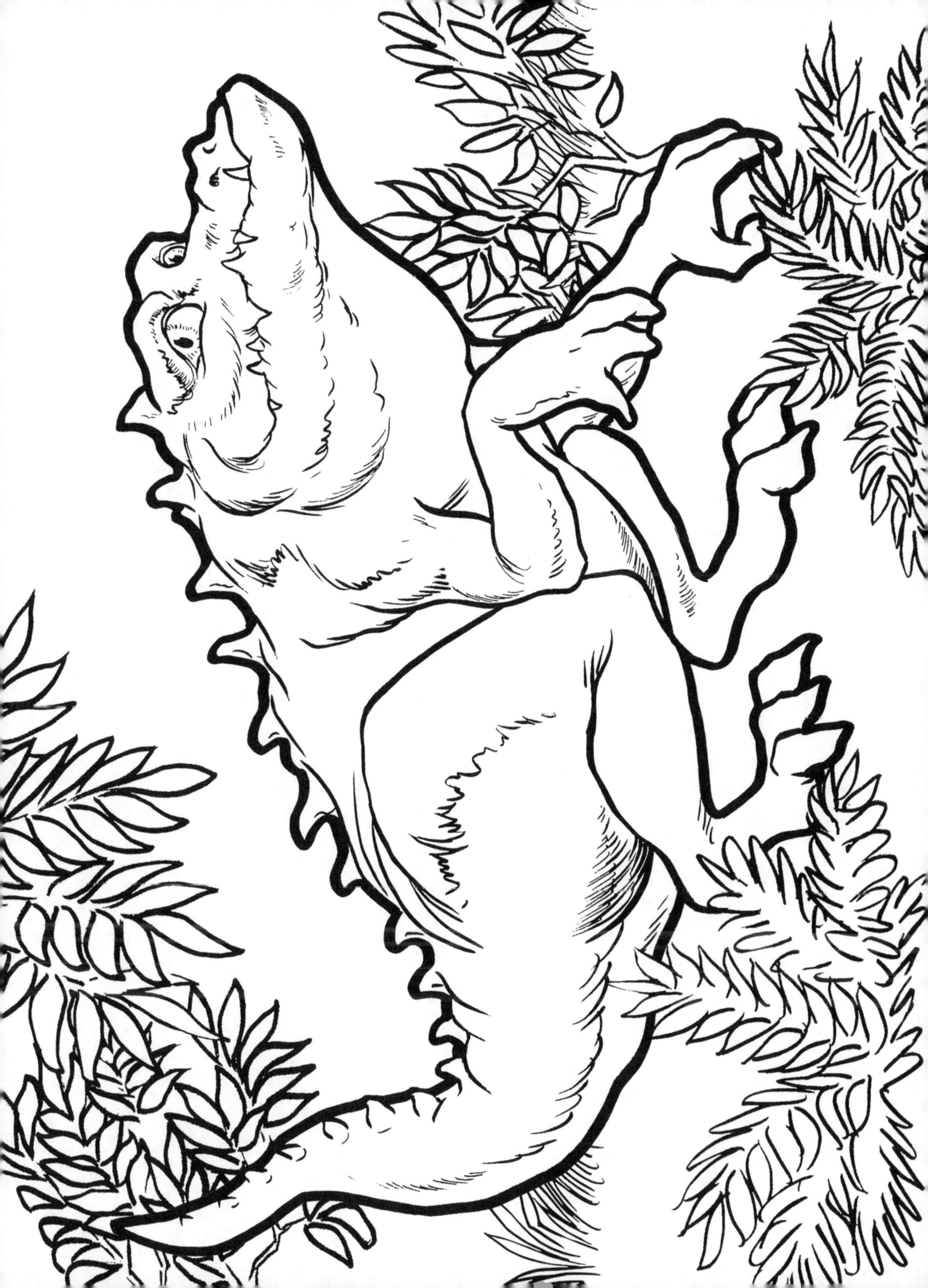

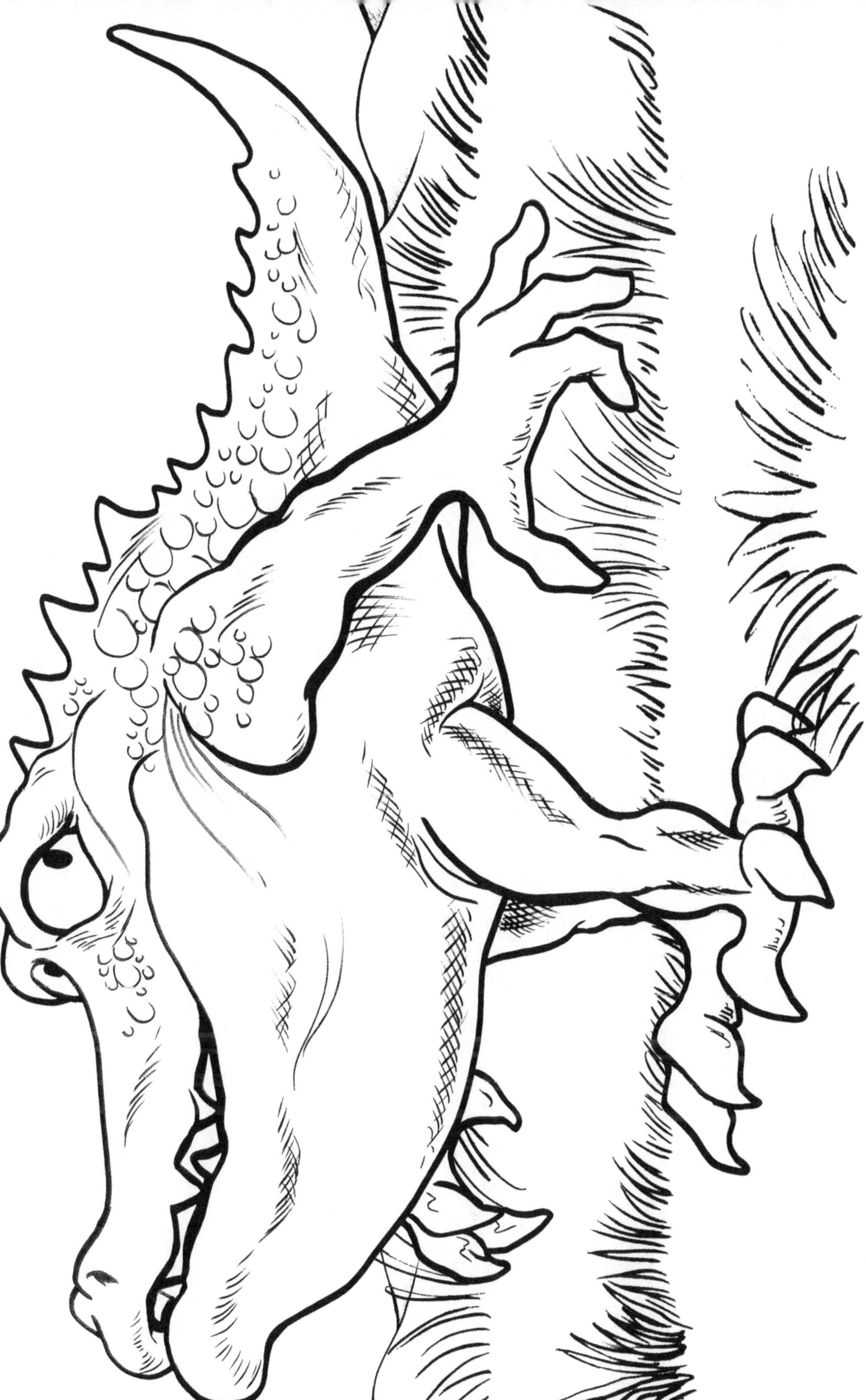

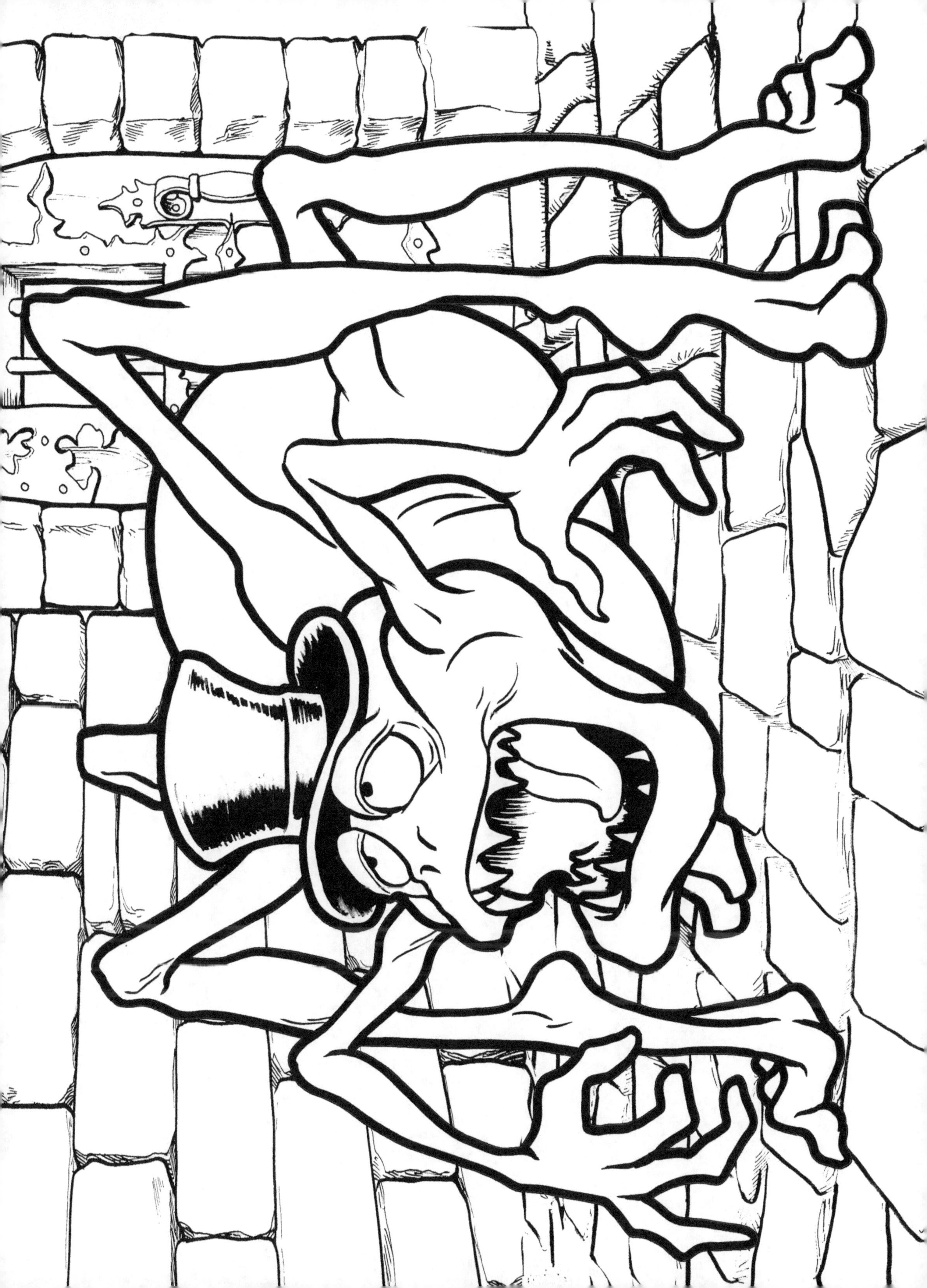

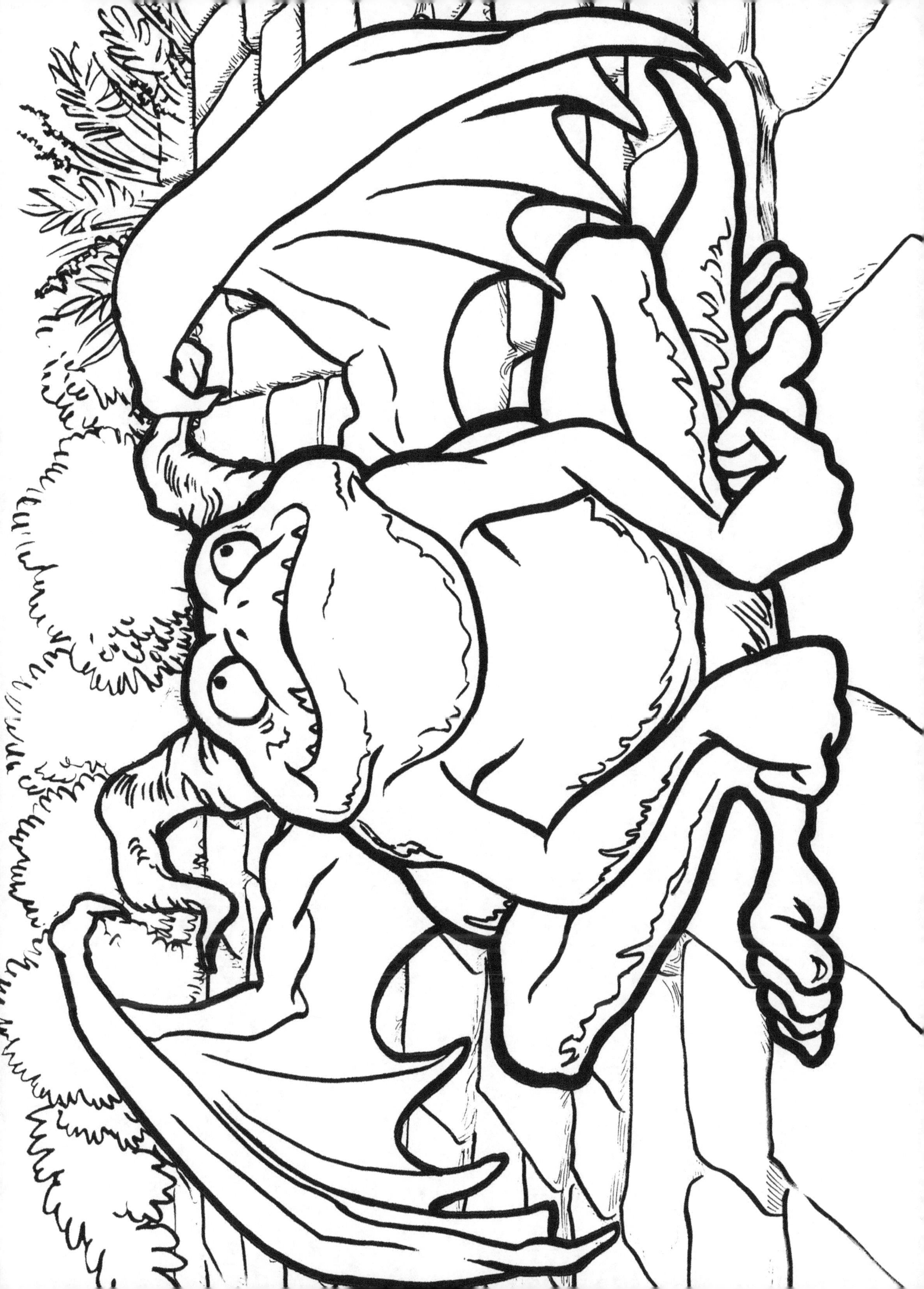

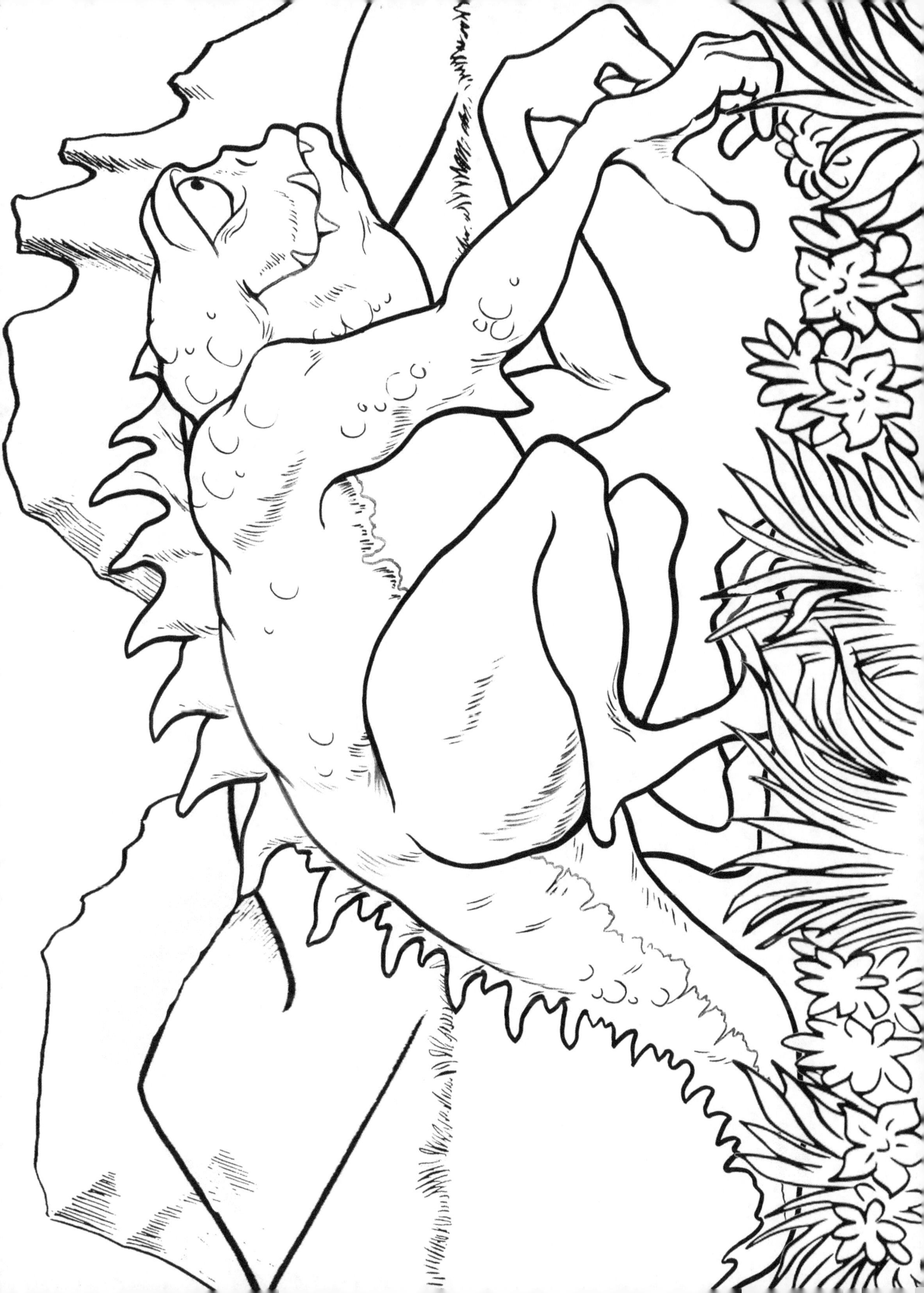

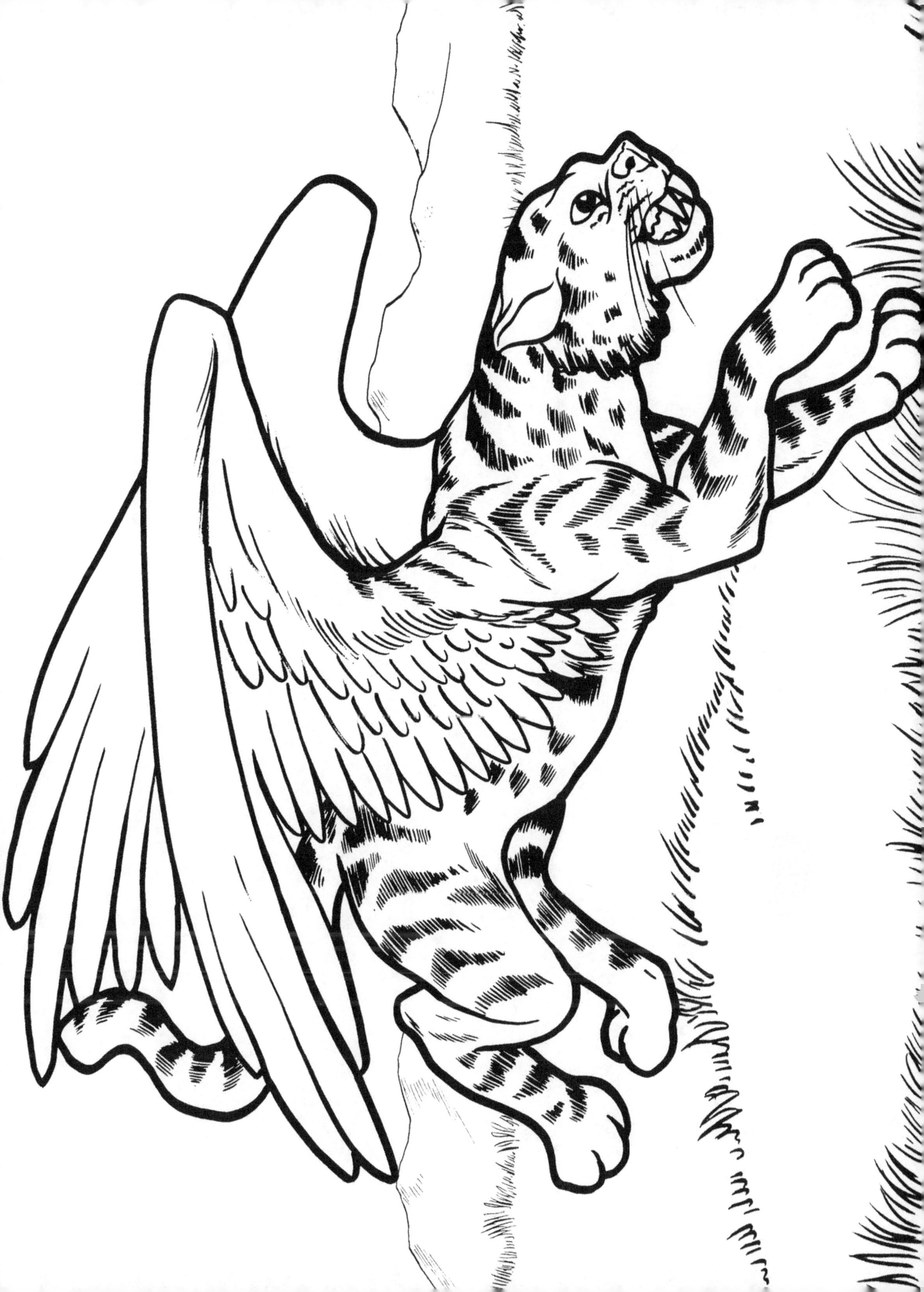

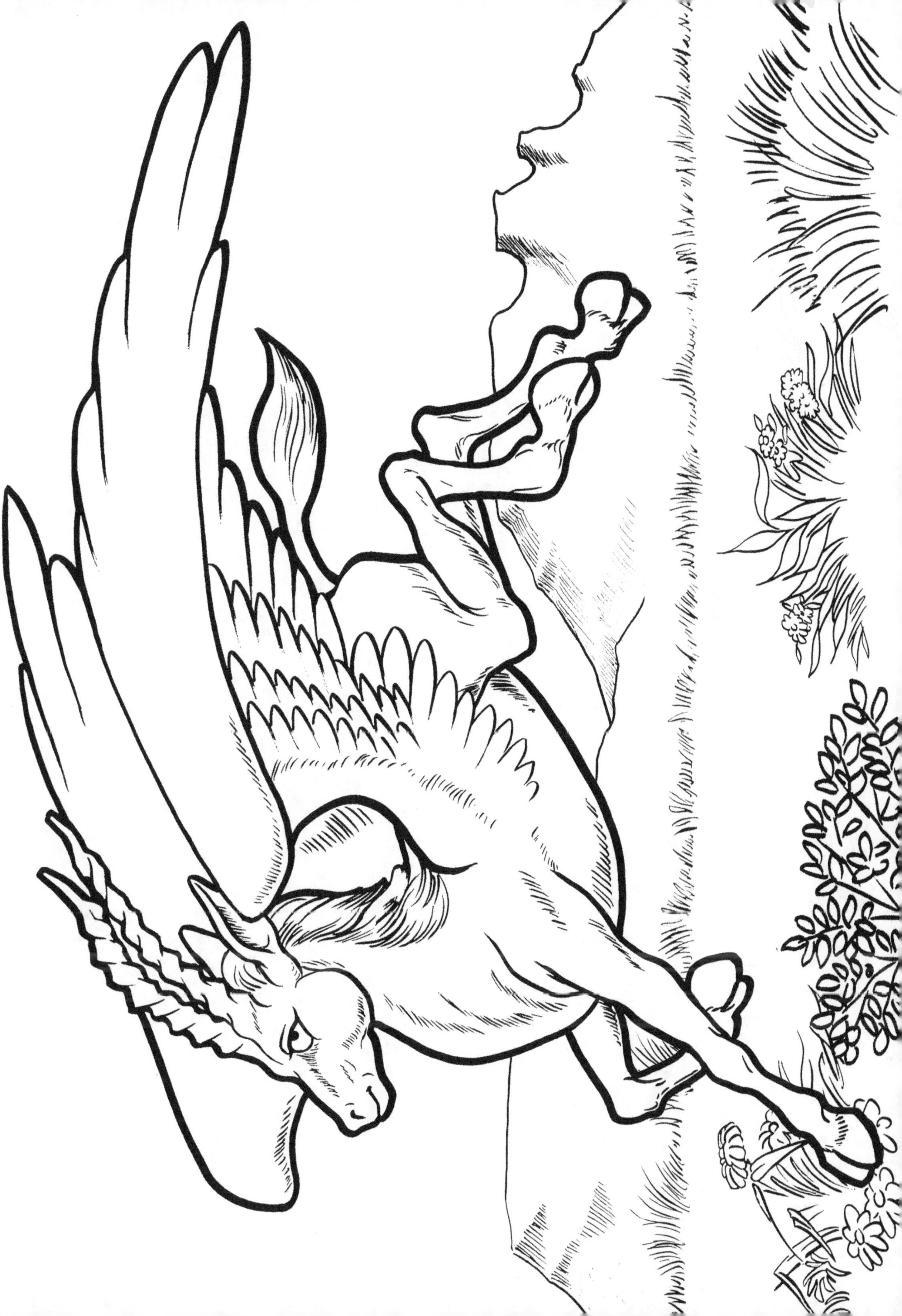

www.ingramcontent.com/pod-product-compliance
Lightning Source LLC
Chambersburg PA
CBHW080612180526
45168CB00007B/2886
9781508553656